THe VERY SAME MOON

PAGE PUBLISHING
Conneaut Lake, PA

First originally published by Page Publishing 2023

ISBN 979-8-88654-801-3 (pbk)
ISBN 979-8-88654-802-0 (digital)

Printed in the United States of America

THE VERY SAME MOON

Jeanine Faietta Eastman

The very same moon shines on the lake
like a glow stick, perfect and bright.
The light never stops glowing all through the night!

This is the very same moon that Peyton's
great-nana loved to see. So many
years ago, how can that be?

Well, the very same moon is cozy and safe,
high in the sky, in its own special place.
When you look up high, it's so good to
know the moon is the same wherever
you go! The moon never ever changes even as
years pass by, never to fade or go astray.
The very same moon is the same
tomorrow as it was yesterday.

The lakeside tree is full of wonder in the
early-morning hours of the day. Green, prickly
branches, so be careful when you touch!
Standing tall and proud and putting a smile
on everyone's face. You have found your home,
lakeside tree, in the most perfect place!

The days are getting shorter; darkness will be rolling in soon. The lakeside tree stays bundled up with a coat of soft, green fir, excitedly saying good night to the day as the very same moon tops it off in the most magical way!

The deer friends graze on the snowy glaze,
born to travel in herds for days! Wild and free,
that's the way it should be! By staying together,
it keeps them warm and cozy during the
cold Maine weather. Deer find shelter among
the pine trees. This is why Maine is
the perfect place for them to be. After all,
Maine is the Pine Tree State. How do the
deer know this? Wow, they sure are great!
The very same moon has been guiding the
herd with a sparkling moonbeam so bright.
To infinity, the light will never end or change.
It's been the same since the very first night!

The frozen lake is as clear as glass as far as the
eye can see! Tie up your skates and put on
a show for the lakeside tree! When the north
wind blows, it is so freezing cold. Bundle
up from your head to your toes, or icicles
will start growing from your nose. If you
get tired, take a rest. Sit down on the ice
and put your snow pants to the test!

The days are getting longer; spring is in the air. The frozen lake is crackling like thunder. Chunks of ice are everywhere! Soon the ice will be gone, on its merry way. I wonder what all the fish will say as they swim around in their schools? Surely, they will be over the moon. After all, they're no fools!

The very same moon is hiding out in the daytime sky, keeping watch over the lake as the ice chunks float by. The light on the wavy lake water is once again gleaming. Mother Nature thinks she is dreaming. Spring is here to stay!

After a spring storm, a rainbow is born—
bursts of color in the sky. The promise of
sunshine after the rain surely will not pass us
by! Look up to the magical arch while you
still have the chance. You'll be so glad you
did; it will make you do the happy dance!
The rainbow will slowly fade and drift away,
leaving a stream of glitter in the sky.
Have no fear; magic will again be here
when another storm passes by!

The very same moon never fades away,
hanging out in the night sky, holding on
to all that glimmer. Count your lucky stars.
The very same moon will never be dimmer!

The eagle is a fearless high flyer as she
soars through the sky, over the lake to a
nest nearby. Perched on top of the tree, the
nest is so large, built using sticks, grass,
and twigs with the eagle in charge! The eagle's
great wingspan is a sight to behold as
she swoops in the water, looking for fish.
With powerful eyesight, she is sure to get
her wish!
Mom and dad eagles are so nurturing,
taking such loving care of their young,
tucking them into their cozy nest when the day
is done. Last night when it was dark and maybe
a little scary; the very same moon shined over
the eaglets' bed. The lights will glimmer for days,
but not too bright for the little sleepyheads!
Eagles stand fierce and proud—a symbol of
freedom and peace shared with us all!

Mr. Duck and Myrtle the Turtle are such good
friends, sunbathing on the rocks until
the day's end. When the sky grows dark and
the clouds roll in, the very same moon
is at it again! A glistening light high from
the sky appears out of the darkness in
the blink of an eye!
Myrtle the Turtle may swim a bit slower
than Mr. Duck, going back to the shore.
Her standards are not any lower; she does just
fine, keeping up! The friends make it back
to the lake shore, wearing their built-in life
jackets. Could they ask for anything more?
Just for another fun day together
tomorrow with so much to explore!

As dusk settles in, Peyton's uncle and papa take
a paddle ride in the red canoe, going on a
great adventure. Will they see a loon or two?
Or the great blue heron? Myrtle the Turtle or
Mr. Duck? Perhaps the eagle, with any luck!
The waters are peaceful and calm, but safety first
with their life jackets on. Using the paddle to guide
the canoe is lots of hard work but so fun to do.
It's starting to grow a bit darker, but no need to be
afraid. They have nature's flashlight, custom-made!
Thank you to the very same moon for making a
way home, sweet lake for another great day!

From dusk to dawn every summer, the call of
the loon sounds so crazy, shouting, "Wake up,
Highland Lake! Why are you being so lazy?"
Many love to hear the call of the loon each and
every day. The loons are letting us
know they are here to stay!
Did you know that every boy loon sings a
different tune? Amazing! They even have their
own boy band and perform for
the very same moon!
When dusk rolls in, the very same moon
is reminded how grateful to be for all
of the loon friends! And the moon danced the
night away to the loon's boy band. A standing
ovation was at hand. Suddenly a perfect
glow shined down from the night, leading
the loons home with shining spotlights!

Autumn is calling; summer has waved us
goodbye. The deer friends are jumping
through the colorful, crunchy leaves, flying
and swirling in the crisp autumn breeze.
Born to be social, they love to play. Deer
just want to have fun on any giving day!
The deer friends also work hard, looking for food
from dusk until dawn, with their sharp eyesight
leading them along. The sun is going to need a
nap; the very same moon will have a turn to shine!
Guiding the herd's path, darkness will be
gone. The night sky will be so bright, the
deer will need their sunglasses on!
Although winter is near, they never fear. Cozy fur
coats are a perfect fit for each and every deer!

The autumn leaves have gathered on the ground.
They look so sad, just lying around. Grab
your rake and make a huge pile. Jump on in
and stay for a while! When springtime arrives,
new leaves will bloom. The tree limbs are
empty, so there is plenty of room!
The leaves may change color and fall to the
ground. As always, the very same moon can
still be found—high in the sky, glowing
so bright, not known to be shy! Forever
and always as the years go by!

The great blue heron is stunning to see, flying
through the air at rapid speed! With wings
so long and legs so high, no wonder her nest nearly
touches the sky! The heron is a pro at catching
lots of different fishes. She stands for hours so
patiently and waits, bringing home a good catch
to cook up some new dishes! While she's flying
home to the nest, soon it will start to get dark.
The great blue heron never worries; that would
give her wrinkles. She is certain the very same
moon has plugged in strings and
strings of lights that twinkle!

No matter where you live, the place you call
home, or even if you may roam, when you
look up at the night sky, you will see the moon.
Think of someone special you love, near
or far. Maybe someone from long ago that you
have never even met. You can bet this is
true: they have looked up at the very same moon
as you! Our moon never changes, hanging
above in the heavenly sky. It always stays the
same as infinity passes by. Full of comfort, peace,
and love, our moon will never make you blue.
The very same moon will always be there
for you, guiding you along the way with a
magnificent light since the very first night.

About the Author

Jeanine Faietta Eastman was born and raised in the great state of Maine. She lives with her family on Highland Lake, where she loves to explore and capture beautiful photos of nature and the animals all around her. The wonderful illustrations are derived from her photos. Jeanine also enjoyed refurbishing her vintage camper which is featured on the book's cover. Since childhood, she has cherished the beauty and wonder of the lake's waters and the night sky just as generations of her family before and after her through every season of life.

The Very Same Moon is Jeanine's first published children's book. She would like you to meet her neighbors: the loons, the majestic bald eagles, her deer friends, and many more! All rely on the very same moon to guide them home. She hopes *The Very Same Moon* makes you smile, do the happy dance, and maybe even have a few icicles growing out of your nose, if you're lucky! All while it comforts you, bringing peace to your heart with its guiding, glistening light just like it has since the very first night.

9 798886 548013